A/CD/11

Problems —
Proofreader Crashes

CONTENTS

ILLUSTRATIONS

INTRODUCTION

Charles Dickens was born on 7th February 1812 and died on 9th June 1870. This book tells the story of Dickens's links with Southwark, using where possible the novelist's own words. Southwark can rightly claim a special place in the hearts of lovers of Dickens. Mrs Boger wrote in her book *Bygone Southwark*, published in 1895, '....there is scarcely a part of old Southwark that Dickens has not touched upon either in his life or his works.'

The Southwark that Dickens knew particularly well was 'The Borough', the neighbourhood of Borough High Street. He was, however, also acquainted with many other parts of the present London Borough of Southwark, an area which covers a large area between London Bridge and Crystal Palace.

This booklet can only give a glimpse of the world of Charles Dickens, but we hope that it will encourage those interested to make further discoveries.

LODGINGS IN LANT STREET

As a boy, Dickens came to know Southwark well. His father, John Dickens, was heavily in debt and the efforts of Mrs Dickens to found a scholastic establishment at their house in Gower Street proved a failure. Nearly everything in the house went to the pawnbrokers and the elder Dickens was imprisoned in the Marshalsea Debtors Prison in Borough High Street to be followed soon after by Mrs Dickens and all the children except Charles and Fanny.

According to John Forster, Dickens's friend and biographer, however, 'they had no want of bodily comfort there. His father's income, still going on, was amply sufficient for that - the family lived more comfortably in prison than they had done for a long time out of it.'

Young Charles, at the age of twelve, was found work at a blacking factory at Hungerford Stairs, at the wage of six shillings a week and moved to lodgings in Lant Street on the west of Borough High Street, with Archibald Russell, an Agent for the Insolvent Court. It was near enough to the Marshalsea to take breakfast and supper with his parents. On his way to and from work, through the notorious Mint district of Southwark he must have noted many unsavoury or colourful characters and squalid scenes which he later turned to good account in his novels. It is believed for example, that his description of a workhouse in *Oliver Twist* was based on the old St George's Workhouse in Mint Street. Although for Dickens a period of deepest misery, he was at least fortunate in his lodgings.

As he wrote later,

> 'A back attic was found for me at the house of an 'Insolvent-court agent' who lived in Lant Street in the Borough where Bob Sawyer lodged many years afterwards. A bed and bedding were sent over for me and made up on the floor. The little window had a pleasant prospect of a timber yard, and when I took possession of my new abode, I thought it was a Paradise.'

Lant Street, 1898

In *The Pickwick Papers* there is a vivid description of the Lant Street neighbourhood.

'There is a repose about Lant Street in the Borough which sheds a gentle melancholy upon the soul. There are also a good many houses to let in this street, it is a bye street too, and its dullness is soothing...In this happy retreat are colonised a few clear-starchers, a sprinkling of journeymen bookbinders, one or two prison agents for the Insolvent Court, several small housekeepers who are employed in the docks, a handful of mantua makers and a seasoning of jobbing tailors. The majority of the inhabitants either direct their energies to the letting of furnished apartments or devote themselves to the healthful and invigorating pursuit of mangling. The chief features in the still life of the street are green shutters, lodging-bills, brass door-plate handles; the principal specimens of animated nature, the pot-boy, the muffin youth and the baked-potato man. The population is migratory, usually disappearing on the verge of quarter-day and generally by night. His Majesty's revenues are seldom collected in this happy valley, the rents are dubious and the water communication is very frequently cut off.'

Bob Sawyer, a medical student at Guy's Hospital, 'a carver and cutter of live people's bodies' had lodgings not far away in Lant Street. He had a party there one night which became somewhat riotous and resulted in the landlady ordering the guests, one of whom was Mr Pickwick, to leave. Ben Allen 'made the best of his way back, knocked double knocks at the door of the Borough Market Office and took short naps on the step alternately, until daybreak, under the firm impression that he lived there and had forgotten the key.'

Lant Street still exists and a school built originally for the London School Board in 1877, is now Charles Dickens Primary School. Nearby streets have been named Weller Street, Pickwick Street, Quilp Street, Dorrit Street and Copperfield Street.

LONDON BRIDGE

The literary pilgrim who enjoys following in the footsteps of Dickens and his characters could well make a start at London Bridge. Little Dorrit, Mrs Clennam, Barnaby Rudge and Mr Plornish amongst others, all passed over London Bridge. In some novels the bridge referred to is that designed by John Rennie and opened in 1831, which has now been transported to America and replaced by the new bridge. On other occasions Dickens is obviously remembering the old London Bridge of his youth. This bridge dated from the Middle Ages, although by Dickens's time the houses which formerly lined it had already been removed.

London Bridge, seen from the tower of Southwark Cathedral, 1833

In *Great Expectations* Pip crossed the old London Bridge in agonies of despair after hearing that Estella was to be married to Drummle. The same bridge was David Copperfield's favourite lounging place.

> 'I was wont to sit, in one of the stone recesses watching the people going by, or to look over the balustrades at the sun shining in the water and lighting up the golden flame on top of the Monument.'

One of the niches has been preserved in the grounds of Guy's Hospital.

At this period Mr and Mrs Micawber were in the King's Bench Prison in Borough High Street and young David was working in the bottle factory.

It was whilst accompanying the Pickwickians to London Bridge on their way home from Bob Sawyer's party that Ben Allen confided to Mr Winkle that 'he was resolved to cut the throat of any gentlemen, except Mr Bob Sawyer, who should aspire to the affections of his sister Arabella.'

It was the 1831 bridge which Dickens had in mind when writing *Oliver Twist* and the steps which used to lead down the river to the west of the bridge were known as "Nancy's Steps". According to the novel the fateful meeting between Nancy and Mr Brownlow took place at a flight of steps on the Surrey bank on the same side of the bridge against St Saviour's Church (now Southwark Cathedral). Dickens knew precisely how it was possible for Noah Claypole to conceal himself and overhear Nancy warning them of Oliver's danger.

> 'These stairs are part of the bridge; they consist of three flights. Just below the end of the second, going down, the stone wall on the left terminates in an ornamental pilaster facing towards the Thames. At this point the lower steps widen so that a person turning the angle of the wall is necessarily unseen by any others on the stairs who chance to be above him, if only a step.'

The tide was out and thus it was that Claypole was enabled to carry out his treacherous task unseen. Claypole's disclosure of what he had heard led ultimately to Nancy's brutal murder at the hands of Bill Sikes.

To return for a moment to the meeting of Nancy and Rose.

'A mist hung over the river, deepening the red glare of fires that burnt upon the small craft moored off the different wharfs and rendering darker and more indistinct the murky buildings on the banks. The old smoke-stained storehouses on either side rose heavy and dull from the dense mass of roofs and gables and frowned sternly upon water too black to reflect even their lumbering shapes. The tower of old Saint Saviour's Church and the spire of St Magnus, so long the giant warders of the ancient bridge, were visible in the gloom; but the forest of shipping below the bridge and the thickly scattered spires of churches above them were nearly all hidden from sight.'

SOUTHWARK CATHEDRAL

In the chapter on the "City of London Churches" in *The Uncommercial Traveller* Dickens disclaims knowledge of the names of many of the churches he visited. But he says, 'I know the church of old Gower's tomb (he lies in effigy with his head upon his books) to be the church of St Saviour's, Southwark.'

In 1905 St Saviour's became Southwark Cathedral. Overman's Almshouses, adjacent to Southwark Cathedral, may have been in Dickens's mind when he describes the almshouses that David Copperfield

Southwark Cathedral, c. 1838

visited before taking the coach on the final stage of the journey to Salem House School at Blackheath. David had been met at an inn in Whitechapel by Mr Mell, an assistant schoolmaster.

'We went on through a great noise and an uproar that confused my weary head beyond description and over a bridge which, no doubt was London Bridge...until we came...to some almshouses as I knew by their look, and by an inscription on a stone over the gate which said they were established for twenty-five poor women.'

Overman's Almshouses were actually for eight women. The almshouses are described as having little black doors which were all alike, each having a little diamond-pained window above. Here, David was introduced to Mr Mell's old mother who cooked him a breakfast. Mr Mell, meanwhile, played the flute to his mother and Mrs Fibbitson to their great enjoyment. The almshouses were demolished in 1830 but there is still a memorial in the Cathedral to the Overman family.

THE INNS OF BOROUGH HIGH STREET

In *Pickwick Papers* Dickens describes the famous old inns which formerly lined Borough High Street.

'In the Borough especially there still remain some half-dozen old inns which have preserved their external features unchanged and which have escaped the rage for public improvement and the encroachments of private speculation. Great rambling, queer, old places they are, with galleries and staircases, wide enough and antiquated enough to furnish materials for a hundred ghost stories, supposing we should ever be reduced to the lamentable necessity of inventing any, and that the world should exist long enough to exhaust the innumerable veracious legends connected with old London Bridge and its adjacent neighbourhood on the Surrey side.'

Today the George alone survives, now the only galleried inn left in London. Although typically Dickensian, the only specific reference to it appears in Little Dorrit where Maggy speaking of Tip says '....if he goes into the George and writes a letter....' Theories have been advanced that

Dickens had in mind the George for certain of the scenes in Pickwick, but such controversy makes matters unnecessarily complicated as Dickens himself mentions only the White Hart.

It was at the White Hart, the largest of the coaching inns, demolished in 1889, that Mr Pickwick first encountered Sam Weller. After chasing the eloping couple, Rachel and Jingle from Dingley Dell, Pickwick and Wardle arrived at the yard of the White Hart where they encountered Sam,

Yard of the White Hart Inn, Borough High Street, 1829

> 'burnishing a pair of painted tops (boots), the personal property of a farmer who was refreshing himself with a slight lunch of two or three pounds of beef and a pot or two of por- ter, after the fatigues of the Borough Market.'

The inn yard is then described.

> 'It presented none of that bustle and activity which are the usual characteristics of a large coaching inn. Three or four lumbering waggons, each with a pile of goods beneath its ample canopy about the height of a second floor window of an ordinary house, were stowed away beneath a lofting which extended over one end of the yard; and another, which was to commence its journey in the morning, was drawn out into an open space. A double tier of bedroom galleries with old clumsy balustrades ran round two sides of the straggling area, and a double row of bells to correspond, sheltered from the weather by a little

sloping roof, hung over the door leading to the bar and coffee room. Two or three gigs or chaise-carts were wheeled up under different little sheds and pent houses....a loud ringing of one of the bells was followed by the appearance of a smart chambermaid in the upper sleeping gallery, who after tapping at one of the doors and receiving a request from within, called over the balustrade.'

'The bustling landlady of the White Hart made her appearance in the opposite gallery, and after a little vituperation, flung a pair of lady's shoes into the yard and bustled away.'

All that is left to remind us of the White Hart is the inn yard leading off Borough High Street.

LITTLE DORRIT'S CHURCH

St. George the Martyr Church, 1814

St George the Martyr, in Borough High Street at the junction with Long Lane and Tabard Street, built in 1734 on the site of an earlier church, is sometimes known as "Little Dorrit's Church".

Little Dorrit who was born in the nearby Marshalsea Prison was christened at St George's. One night when she returned too late and was locked out of the Marshalsea Prison she slept in the vestry with the church register for a pillow. It was later at this same church that she was married to Arthur Clennam, the bridal couple pausing on the steps 'looking at the fresh perspective of the street in the autumn morning sun's bright rays'. In the bottom right-hand corner of the modern stained-glass window at the east end of the church is a representation of Little Dorrit wearing a poke bonnet.

THE PRISONS

The old Marshalsea Prison in Borough High Street which closed in 1842 was well known to Dickens from his own boyhood. Much of the first part of *Little Dorrit* revolves around it. In 1856 Dickens wrote:

> 'Thirty years ago there stood, a few doors on the left-hand side of the way going southward, the Marshalsea Prison. It had stood there many years before and remained there some years afterwards, but it is gone now and the world is none the worse without it. It was an oblong pile of barrack building, partitioned into squalid houses standing back to back, so that there were no back rooms; environed by a narrow paved yard, hemmed in by high walls duly spiked at the top. Itself a close and confined prison for debtors, it contained within it a much closer and more confined gaol for smugglers. Offenders against the revenue laws, and defaulters to excise and customs, who had incurred fines which they were unable to pay, were supposed to be incarcerated behind an iron-plated door, closing up a second prison, consisting of a strong cell or two, and a blind alley some yard and a half wide, which formed the mysterious termination of the very limited skittleground in

which the Marshalsea debtors bowled down their troubles. Supposed to be incarcerated there, because the time had rather outgrown the strong cells and the blind alley, in practice they had come to be considered a little too bad, though in theory they were quite as good as ever.....hence the smugglers habitually consorted with the debtors (who received them with open arms), except at certain constitutional moments when somebody came from some office, to go through some form of overlooking something, which neither he nor anybody else knew anything about.'

Wall of the Marshalsea Prison 1877

Little Dorrit was issued in monthly parts between 1856 and 1857. In his preface to the completed work Dickens wrote:

'Some of my readers may have an interest in being informed whether or no any portions of the Marshalsea Prison are yet standing. I myself did not know, until I was approaching the end of this story, when I went to look. I found the outer front court-yard, often mentioned here, metamorphosed into a butter shop; and I then almost gave up every brick of the jail for lost. Wandering, however, down a certain adjacent Angel Court, leading to Bermondsey, I came to Marshalsea Place the houses in which I recognised, not only as the great block of the former prison, but as preserving the rooms that arose in my mind's eye when I became Little Dorrit's biographer. The smallest boy I ever conversed with, carrying the largest baby I ever saw, offered a supernaturally intelligent explanation of the locality in its old uses and was very nearly correct. How this young Newton came by this information, I don't know: he was a quarter of a century too young to know anything about it of himself. I pointed to the window of the room where Little Dorrit was born and where her father lived so long and asked him what was the name of the lodger who tenanted that apartment at present. He said, "Tom Pythick". I asked him who was Tom Pythick and he said, "Joe Pythick's uncle".'

'A little further on, I found the older and smaller wall, which used to enclose the pent-up inner prison where nobody was put, except for ceremony. Whosoever goes into Marshalsea Place, turning out of Angel Court, leading to Bermondsey will find his feet on the very paving stones of the extinct Marshalsea jail; will see its narrow yard to the right and to the left, very little altered if at all, except that the walls were lowered when the place got free; will look upon the rooms in which the debtors lived; will stand among the crowding ghosts of many miserable years.'

Today, the only remnant of the old prison is the wall adjacent to Southwark Local Studies Library. The Marshalsea Prison pump is in the Cuming Museum.

The King's Bench Prison occupied a site known as Stones End near the junction of the present Borough Road and Borough High Street. Nicholas Nickleby, searching for the home of the Brays, was directed to a

> 'row of mean and not over-cleanly houses situated within "the rules" of the King's Bench Prison and not many hundred paces distant from the obelisk in St George's Fields.'

> 'The rules were a certain liberty adjoining the prison and comprising some dozen streets in which debtors who could raise money to pay large fees, from which their creditors did not derive any benefit, were permitted to reside.'

Nicholas eventually reached it

> 'after traversing a very dirty and dusty suburb, of which minor theatricals, shell fish, ginger-beer, spring vans, greengrocery and brokers' shops appeared to compose the main and most prominent features.....There were small gardens in front which, being wholly neglected in all other respects, served as little pens for the dust to collect in.....'

David Copperfield's landlord, Mr Micawber, was imprisoned for debt in the King's Bench. David went to dine with him in his room and on Mrs Micawber's joining her husband used to breakfast with them there.

Recrossing Borough High Street and travelling south, the site of Horsemonger Lane Gaol is reached. It stood near the present Inner London Crown Court in Harper Road. Harper Road was formerly Union Road and before that Horsemonger Lane. This was the County Gaol for Surrey, its walls enclosing an area of some three and a half acres and providing accommodation for over four hundred prisoners.

On the morning of 13th November 1849 Dickens witnessed the dreadful scenes accompanying the public hanging for murder of the two Mannings, husband and wife, for the murder of their lodger. Opposite the gaol was a row of tenements in Bath Terrace, a road which still exists today although the tenements have been demolished. The tenants of these houses used to let their rooms to spectators on the day of execution, and did excellent business at such times, often making more than their annual rental.

Dickens was so horrified at the behaviour of the crowds that he was moved to write his famous letter to *The Times* next day commencing,

> 'I do not believe that any community can prosper where such a scene of horror and demoralisation as was enacted this morning outside Horsemonger Lane Gaol is presented at the very doors of good citizens and is passed by, unknown or forgotten.'

It was to be another twenty years before public outcry finally resulted in the abolition of public executions. The gaol was demolished in 1879. The Manning tombstones are now in the Cuming Museum, the museum of Southwark's history, at 155-157 Walworth Road, SE17.

Horsemonger Lane is mentioned in *Little Dorrit*. Here John Chivery, whose father was the turnkey at the Marshalsea Prison, 'assisted his mother in the conduct of a snug tobacco business.'
The shop was a,

> 'rural establishment, one storey high which had the benefit of the air from the yards of Horsemonger Lane Gaol and the advantage of a retired walk under the wall of that pleasant establishment.'

It was decorated with a sign of a Highlander 'on a bracket on the door-post, like a fallen cherub that had found it necessary to take a kilt.' The shop was still standing until 1930.

THE ELEPHANT & CASTLE
AND NEIGHBOURHOOD

Trooper George in *Bleak House* visited a shop in that district of

> 'little shops lying somewhere in that ganglion of roads from
> Kent and Surrey and of streets from the bridges of London,
> centring in the far-famed Elephant who has lost his Castle
> formed of a thousand four-horse coaches, to a stronger iron
> monster than he, ready to chop him into mincemeat any day he
> dares.'

The shop for the sale of musical instruments was kept by Mrs Bagnet
who was 'as usual washing greens. I never saw her, except upon a
baggage wagon, when she wasn't washing greens.'

An incident in *David Copperfield* occurred in the New Kent Road not
far from the Elephant & Castle. When young David decided to make
his way from his lodgings to his Aunt Betsy Trotwood at Dover he
looked around to find someone to carry his small trunk to the coach
office and saw

> '......a long-legged young man with a very little empty
> donkey-cart standing near the obelisk in Blackfriars Road.'

He bargained with him to do the job for a tanner. But he ran off with
the box having also stolen David's last half-guinea. David chased off
in hopeless pursuit until

> 'I came to a stop in the Kent Road, at a terrace with a piece of
> water before it and a great foolish image in the middle blowing
> a dry shell. Here I sat down on a door-step, quite spent with the
> efforts I had already made and with hardly breath enough to cry
> for the loss of my box and half-guinea.'

The terrace referred to was Webb's County Terrace. The piece of water and the image disappeared in the 1880's. To recall the scene a small open space in what is now called the New Kent Road is known as David Copperfield Garden and the Dickens Fellowship has erected a statue there. The nearby Dickens Square has no specific connection with the author.

In *Great Expectations* Pip visits Wemmick's house at Walworth.

> 'It appeared to be a collection of black lanes, ditches and little gardens and to present the aspect of a rather dull retirement. Wemmick's house was a little wooden cottage in the midst of plots of gardens and the top of it was cut out and painted like a battery mounted with guns.'

About this time a greengrocer named Skiffins carried on his business in the Kent Road and it is possible that Dickens named his Miss Skiffins from a sign-board he had seen at the shop.

In the crowded streets of present-day Walworth it is difficult to imagine the Walworth of Dickens' day, described also in *Sketches by Boz: the Black Veil.*

> 'The back part of Walworth, at its greatest distance from town, is a straggling miserable place enough, even in these days; but five and thirty years ago, the greater portion of it was little better than a dreary waste, inhabited by a few scattered people of most questionable character, whose poverty prevented their living in any better neighbourhood or whose pursuits and mode of life rendered its solitude peculiarly desirable.'

SOUTHWARK IRON BRIDGE

Southwark Bridge, c. 1840

The Southwark Bridge of Dickens's time, known as the Iron Bridge, was designed by John Rennie and opened in 1819. It was a toll-bridge until 1866 and was replaced by the present bridge in 1921.

Here John Chivery proposed to Little Dorrit putting 'his penny on the toll plate of the Iron Bridge' and 'looking about him for the well-known and well-beloved figure of Little Dorrit.' For Little Dorrit had said, 'if you go by the Iron Bridge.....there is an escape from the noise of the street.'

It was 'between Southwark Bridge which is of iron and London Bridge which is of stone' that Gaffer Hexam and his daughter Lizzie in *Our Mutual Friend* engaged in their gruesome search for the bodies of river suicides,

> 'at every mooring chain and rope, at every stationary boat, at the offsets from the piers of Southwark Bridge, at the paddles of the river steamboats as they beat the filthy water, at the

floating logs of timber lashed together lying off certain wharfs....'
Near here Dickens himself once acted out a tragi-comic little scene.
One day young Charles was taken ill at the blacking factory and forced
to go home. His father was at this time in the Marshalsea Prison and
Dickens was so ashamed of his own dwelling that when Bob Fagin
insisted on accompanying him home,

> 'after making several efforts to get rid of him, to all of which
> Bob Fagin, in his goodness, was deaf, shook hands with him on
> the steps of a house near the Southwark Bridge, on the Surrey
> Side, making believe that I lived there. As a finishing piece of
> reality in case of him looking back, I knocked at the door, I
> recollect, and asked, when the woman opened it, if it was Mr
> Robert Fagin's house.'

BLACKFRIARS ROAD

When as a boy Dickens was in lodgings in Lant Street he went daily by
way of Blackfriars Road and the Blackfriars Bridge to his work at the
blacking factory across the river.

> 'My usual way home was over Blackfriars Bridge and down
> that turning in Blackfriars Road (Union Street) which has
> Rowland Hill's chapel on one side and the likeness of a golden
> dog licking a golden pot over a shop door on the other.'

The old Surrey Chapel is no more, but the sign of the Dog and Pot can
now be seen at the Cuming Museum.

Surrey Theatre, Blackfriars Road, 1828

At the St George's Circus end of Blackfriars Road stood the obelisk, erected in 1771, a noted landmark as Dickens wrote in *Christmas Stories: Somebody's Luggage:*

> 'Those that are acquainted with London are aware of a locality on the Surrey side of the River Thames called the Obelisk or, more generally, the Obstacle.'

Southwark was in Surrey before the formation of the County of London in 1889. Dickens had known the neighbourhood since boyhood as he went to a house near the obelisk to have his clothes valued when his father was imprisoned in the Marshalsea. A debtor had to disclose all wearable effects of himself and his family. The obelisk was removed in 1905 to its present position in Lambeth Road near the Imperial War

Museum.

In Blackfriars Road, near the obelisk, was the old Surrey Theatre. It is possible that Dickens had in mind this this theatre as the one in which Frederick Dorrit played the clarinet in the orchestra.

Performances of Dickens's works used to take place in this theatre during his lifetime to wildly enthusiastic audiences. In November 1838, only a month after the issue of the last instalment, a Surrey Theatre playbill records a dramatised production of *Oliver Twist*. Other productions included *Nicholas*

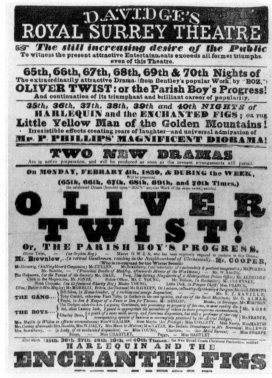

Playbill for the performance of *Oliver Twist* at the Surrey Theatre, 1839

Nickleby. John Forster relates how 'one version at the Surrey Theatre was so excruciatingly bad that in the middle of the first scene the agonised novelist lay down on the floor of his box and never rose until the curtain fell.'

In earlier times the neighbourhood of St George's Circus had been literally St George's Fields. In *Barnaby Rudge* Dickens gives a graphic description of the scenes when Lord George Gordon mustered his anti-Catholic mob in St George's Fields during the notorious riots of 1780.

JACOB'S ISLAND AND THE RIVERSIDE

The temptation to quote at length from *Oliver Twist* cannot be resisted so brilliantly does Dickens paint the scene and so great is the contrast with modern times. There is a particularly vivid description of the riverside neighbourhood formerly known as Jacob's Island which lay to the east of the present site of Tower Bridge, built in 1894:

'Near to that part of the Thames on which the church at Rotherhithe abuts, where the buildings on the banks are dirtiest, and the vessels on the river blackest with the dust of colliers and the smoke of close-built low-roofed houses, there exists......the filthiest, the strangest, the most extraordinary of the many localities that are hidden in London, wholly unknown, even by name, to the great mass of its inhabitants.'

'To reach this place, the visitor has to penetrate through a maze of close, narrow and muddy streets, thronged by the roughest and poorest of water-side people......The cheapest and least delicate provisions are heaped in the shops; the coarsest and commonest of wearing apparel dangle at the salesman's door and stream from the house parapet and windows. Jostling with unemployed labourers of the lowest class, ballast-heavers, coal-whippers, brazen women, ragged children and the very raff and refuse of the river....assailed by offensive sights and smells from the narrow alleys which branch of on the right and left, and deafened by the clash of ponderous wagons that bear great piles of merchandise from the stocks of warehouses that rise from every corner. Arriving, at length, in streets remoter and less frequented than those he had passed (Sikes) walks beneath tottering house-fronts projecting over the pavement, dismantled walls that seem to totter as he passes, chimneys half crushed, half hesitating to fall, windows guarded by rusty iron bars that time and dirt have almost eaten away, and every imaginable sign of desolation and neglect.'

Folly Ditch, Jacob's Island, c. 1850

'In such a neighbourhood beyond Dockland, in the Borough of Southwark, stands Jacob's Island, surrounded by a muddy ditch, six or eight feet deep, and fifteen or twenty wide when the tide is in, once called Mill Pond, but known these days as Folly Ditch. It is a creek or inlet from the Thames and can always be filled at high water by opening the sluices at the lead mills from which it took its old name. At such times a stranger, looking from one of the wooden bridges thrown across it at Mill Lane, will see the inhabitants of the houses on either side lowering, from their back doors and windows, buckets, pails, domestic utensils of all kinds, in which to haul the water up; and when his eye is turned from these operations to the houses themselves, his utmost astonishment will be excited by the scene before him. Crazy wooden galleries common to the backs of half-a-dozen houses, with holes from which to look upon the slime beneath; windows broken and patched, with poles thrust out on which to dry the linen that is never there; rooms so small, so filthy, so confined that the air would seem too tainted even for the dirt and squalor which they shelter; wooden chambers thrusting themselves out above the mud and threatening to fall into it, as some have done; dirt-besmired walls and decaying foundations; every repulsive lineament of poverty, every loathsome indication of filth, rot and garbage - all these ornament the banks of Folly Ditch.'

'In Jacob's Island the warehouses are roofless and empty; the walls are crumbling down; the windows are windows no more; the doors are falling into the streets; the chimneys are blackened, but they yield no smoke....The houses have no owners, they are broken open and entered upon by those who have the courage; and there they live, and there they die. They must have powerful motives for a secret residence, or be reduced to a destitute condition indeed, who seek a refuge in Jacob's Island.'

Southwark Local Studies Library has a deed of 1835, for a house in Eckett Street, owned by the Bridge family, which is traditionally said to be the house that Dickens had in mind for Bill Sikes' lair. Eckett Street was just off Jacob Street which still survives. The Dickens Estate lies just to the east of the site of Eckett Street.

In *The Old Curiosity Shop* Quilp's Wharf is on the Southwark riverside, opposite Quilp's house on Tower Hill. The derelict shipbreaker's yard is described as 'a small, rat-infested, dreary yard....in which were a little wooden counting house....a few fragment of rusty anchors; several large iron rings; some piles of rotten wood and two or three heaps of old sheet-copper.'

Our Mutual Friend provides another glimpse of the riverside,

'the wheels rolled on, and rolled down by the Monument and by the Tower and by the Docks; down by Ratcliff and by Rotherhithe, down by where the accumulated scum of humanity seemed to be washed from higher grounds, like so much moral sewage and to be pausing until its own weight forced it over the bank and sunk it in the river.'

CAMBERWELL, PECKHAM AND NUNHEAD

In *Great Expectations*, Mr Wemmick, Pip's acquaintance, was married to Miss Skiffins at a Camberwell Church.

'We went towards Camberwell Green, and when we were thereabouts, Wemmick said suddenly: "Halloa! Here's a church." There was nothing very surprising in that, but again I was rather surprised when he said "Let's go in!" We went in, Wemmick leaving his fishing rod in the porch and looked all round - "Halloa!" said Wemmick, "Here's Miss Skiffins! Let's have a wedding".'

It is not absolutely certain which church Dickens was suggesting but it was probably Emmanuel Church, Camberwell Road, built in 1842 and closed in 1963. Bishopsmead has been erected on this site.

Horatio Sparkins, an early humorous story in Sketches by Boz, is set in Camberwell. The Maldertons lived at Oak Lodge, Camberwell, where "anyone who could lay claim to an acquaintance with people of rank and title had a sure passport" to their table.

Walter Gay in *Dombey and Son* attended a weekly boarding school in Peckham. There were a number in the neighbourhood in the early nineteenth century.

Dickens rented 16 Linden Grove, Nunhead, for his mistress Ellen Ternan between 1868 and his death in 1870. The house was a substantial Victorian villa, later re-numbered to 31, and was demolished in the early 1970's. Dickens rented the house under the name of Charles Tringham, an alias he had used previously. Ellen Ternan left shortly after Dickens's death.

DULWICH AND MR PICKWICK

Dickens knew Dulwich well as he used to visit the Dulwich Club which met at the Old Greyhound in Dulwich Village opposite the site of the present Crown and Greyhound.

Approaching the end of our survey it is perhaps appropriate to think of the peaceful retirement of Mr Pickwick.

"The house I have taken," said Mr Pickwick, "is at Dulwich. It has a large garden, and is situated in one of the most pleasant spots near London."

There is still a Pickwick Cottage in College Road and this may have been the house which Dickens had in mind.

The Greyhound, Dulwich, c. 1840

The wedding of Mr Snodgrass and Emily Wardle was performed at "Dulwich Church" which, like so many of the churches in Dickens' novels, cannot be certainly identified but was presumably the Old College Chapel. The coaches of the wedding party rattled back to Mr Pickwick's for the wedding breakfast.

At the end of the book Dickens writes,

> 'Mr Pickwick is somewhat infirm now but may still be
> frequently seen, contemplating the pictures in the Dulwich
> Gallery, or enjoying a walk about the pleasant
> neighbourhood....He is known by all the poor people about,
> who never fail to take their hats off, as he passes, with great
> respect. The children idolise him, and so indeed does the whole
> neighbourhood.'

Borough High Street approaching London Bridge, 1827

A SELECTED BIBLIOGRAPHY OF CHARLES DICKENS

THE NOVELS

Most of the novels of Dickens were originally published in serial form; the dates given below are for the complete edition.

1836	Sketches by Boz
1837	Posthumous Papers of the Pickwick Club
1838	Oliver Twist: or, The Parish Boy's Progress
1839	Life and Adventures of Nicholas Nickleby
1841	The Old Curiosity Shop
1841	Barnaby Rudge: A Tale of the Riots of 'Eighty
1843	A Christmas Carol
1844	The Life and Adventures of Martin Chuzzlewit
1848	Dealings with the Firm of Dombey & Son
1850	The Personal History of David Copperfield
1853	Bleak House
1854	Hard Times. For These Times
1857	Little Dorrit
1859	A Tale of Two Cities
1861	The Uncommercial Traveller
1862	Great Expectations
1865	Our Mutual Friend
1870	The Mystery of Edwin Drood (uncompleted)

The novels are available in Penguin with an introduction by Peter Ackroyd. There are very many books on almost every aspect of Dickens's life and work. The following are just a selection, based upon books available thorough Southwark Libraries.

BIOGRAPHY

ACKROYD, P	Dickens. 1990
BROWN, I	Dickens and his world. 1970
CHESTERTON, G K	Charles Dickens
FORSTER, J	The life of Charles Dickens. 2 volumes reprinted 1970
HIBBERT, C	The making of Charles Dickens. 1967
JOHNSON, E	Charles Dickens: his tragedy and triumph. Rev and abridged 1986
PAGE, N	A Dickens chronology. 1988
PAGE, N	A Dickens companion. 1984
POPE-HENNESSEY, U	Charles Dickens, 1812-70 reprinted 1970
PRIESTLY, J B	Charles Dickens and his world. 1969

OTHER WORKS

BELL, A D	London in the age of Dickens. 1967
BROWN, I	Dickens in his time. 1963
FLETCHER, G	Pocket guide to Dickens's London. 1971
GREAVES, J	Who's who in Dickens. 1972
THE LONDON OF CHARLES DICKENS	With a foreward by Monica Dickens (produced by the London Transport Executive and the Dickens Fellowship). 1979
LYNCH, T	Dickens' England: a travellers' companion. 1986
MORELAND, A	Dickens landmarks in London. 1931
PAGE, N	A Dickens chronology. 1988
PAGE, N	A Dickens companion. 1984
SCHWARZBACH, F S	Dickens and the city. 1979
TOMALIN, C	The invisible woman: the story of Nelly Ternan and Charles Dickens. 1990
WILSON, A	The world of Charles Dickens. 1983

Further material on Charles Dickens and Southwark is available at Southwark Local Studies Library, 211 Borough High Street, London SE1 1JA, Telephone 0171 403 3507.

This book was produced by members of the staff of Southwark Libraries. Original text by Graham Prettejohns, Brenda Mann and Larry Ilott, this edition edited by Janice Brooker and Stephen Humphrey.

Produced by Leisure Design